# FINALLY
# FREE!
## I WAS A PRISONER OF MY
## OWN THOUGHTS

Joyce Fleming

# PATASKITY PUBLISHING CO.

Pataskity Publishing Co.
207 Hudson Trce Suite 102
Augusta, GA 30906
pataskitypublishing.com
(706) 250-3956

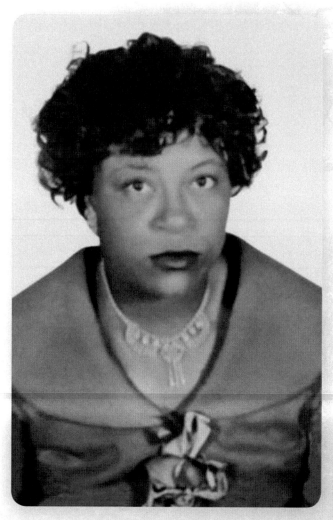

*I dedicate this book in loving memory of my mother,*
*Vileain Gaines Jones.*

*A special thank you to my little brother,*
*Joel.*

*Having you in my life kept me emotionally stable.*
*You were the only one in the house who I really felt*
*connected to.*

# *Acknowledgments*

I could not accomplish all of this alone. I am so grateful to many of you who contributed to my life, for standing by me and encouraging me along the way.

I give God the glory for allowing his angels to watch over me during the most vulnerable years of my life as a child.

I thank my daughter for how she comforted me as a little girl not even realizing she was ministering to my very soul and mind.

To my oldest son who has been a role model for me. Thank you for inspiring me to write this book.

To my baby son whom I love very much! Thank you for the times when you protected me from physical abuse and assisted me when you were a teen from time to time with my computer skills along the way.

To all of my children and grandchildren whom I love and pray for every day! I appreciate each of you for giving me the joy of loving someone more than I thought I ever could.

Brian, thank you for being the wonderful and loving person that I have come to know and love.

To my therapist and doctors that have shown me so much care.

To my brothers and sisters, my father and mother, my foundation and my roots.

To Pataskity Publishing Company, thank you! Ana, I appreciate your help.

To my Literary Agent, Heather, thank you! I appreciate you!

To old and new friends in my life who have loved and encouraged me over the years.

Thank you Ray, my husband and best friend for standing by me, for keeping me balanced, for loving and caring for me, and giving me a home in your heart.

# Contents

# *Preface*

My story began with me being an egg that was transported to my mother's fallopian tube. The egg stayed in the fallopian tube waiting to be fertilized for about three to four days. Within twenty-four hours after being fertilized by my father's sperm, I began to divide fast into many cells, and continued to, as I moved slowly through the fallopian tube to my mother's uterus. After arriving there, I took shelter deep into the lining of her uterus. This is where I stayed until the time of my mother's delivery. I was rejected before I could make my grand entrance into the world. My mother had complications during her delivery with me due to my size and other unknown issues. The doctors felt as though they would not be able to save the both of us. With all of the complications, the situation was out of the doctors' control to save both of us! At that moment, my mother had a choice to make, and she made a decision that she would not abort me. Her request was that the doctor try to save both of us. My mother's faith brought us through!

Sometimes life tries to stop your destiny before you even get here! The interventions that allowed me to enter this world were beyond the doctors or my mother's control. Despite the odds, my mother safely delivered me and I was a healthy baby girl born to James Jones Sr. and Vileain Jones. I, Joyce Annette Jones, was born on Tuesday December 6, 1955, time unknown, a 10 lbs. 11oz baby girl, the sixth child of the Jones' family.

On that day, the maximum temperature was 59.0 F, maximum sustained wind speed 11.62 MPH, and no rain reported. On December 6, 1955, my journey of life began. This world just opened up and sucked me right in. At that time, I was not even aware that the way I would perceive my relationships with my parents would lay the foundation for many failed relationships throughout my lifetime.

While writing this book, I was challenged with thoughts and situations that I did not realize I had buried deep down in my self- conscious mind. As I begin to write down my thoughts and reminisce on my past life, this allowed me the opportunity to come face- to -face with all the good, the bad and the ugly memories of my life and start the healing process of wholeness. Romans 8:28 states, *"All things work together for the good of those who love the Lord;"* Therefore all of my experiences which I have endured contributes to me being who I am today.

# Chapter One
## *The Realization of My Existence*

While I am not sure when the realization of my existence in this world first occurred to me, to this day, I can recall an incident taking place when I was around four or five years old. My baby brother was having problems zipping up his pants. I tried to help him, and my mother noticed me. Then, she asked, *"What are you doing?"* Before I could answer, I remember her hitting me with her belt. I began to cry. I did not understand why I was being beaten for just helping my little brother zip up his pants. I did not ask because I knew I would probably have gotten beaten some more. My mother and father, especially my mother, were very strict in their parenting. My mother was the disciplinary in our home. You had to think before you speak or risk getting knocked down, and I mean it literally.

Growing up in our family at least for me, I was seen but not heard. It was almost like everyone around me was living their life and mine was just standing still. It was like no one even noticed that I was there. I do not remember ever hearing the following statements: *"I love you!" "You did a good job!" "How was your day?" "Come, give me a hug." "I miss you." "You are my little girl!" "You can be anything you want to be!" "I am here to help you along life's way!" "You are not alone!" "If no one else loves you, mommy loves you!"* I do not recall ever being close to my mom when I was growing up, her giving me a hug or even being touched. My only childhood memories of being touched by my mom was to get my hair braided or when I was being disciplined.

I vowed when I was a young girl that I would hug, show and tell my children every day that I loved them and supported them in their lives. In my opinion, everything I did or did not do was under a microscope, and I was going to be blamed for it anyway. My life as a child was scary in some way or another and I was always afraid. I felt alone and left out. If I was not worrying about getting a beating, I was afraid of the rodents or bugs that were constantly moving about in our house. Although I feared the rodents and bugs as most children my age would have, the rodents and bugs seemed to have had more privileges than me. They caused me pure torment! There was a feeling of embarrassment I felt every time kids in the neighborhood would come to our house because our home seemed to have been the worst looking house on the street. I began to have days when I thought to myself, *"something is wrong with me because I lack the attention of my own mommy."* This was a hurtful feeling because I felt rejected. It brought a shyness about me. I grew up feeling like I did not really belong here. I always wondered if I would ever fit in! I grew up in a house where I felt so afraid and alone. I was always afraid of something or someone. I felt as though I would never be good enough. It seemed like my life just stood still, and that I was always in the background while everyone else was living out their lives. Cinderella became my role model because I would watch this show and imagine I was Cinderella. I often imagined that my family was not my biological family, and that a prince would come to rescue me. My fantasy was that one day I would awaken from this bad dream! Although Cinderella was with her step mother and step sisters, being treated like a slave instead of part of the family. She found a way to escape the loneliness and rejection if only in her mind.

One day, Cinderella finally met her Prince Charming; he took her away from this harbor life and gave her the love and care she longed for. In my opinion, my life was similar to Cinderella. No matter what I did, it was not good enough. I often wondered to myself, *"What could I ever do to gain my mother's affection and attention?"* The loneliness, fear, and rejection I experienced as a child led to the wall I self-consciously built in my mind and held myself imprisoned for the majority of my life. I often fed off of pain, disappointments and fear. I spent a lot of time focusing on past situations, choices and events that took place in my life wishing I could go back to a place in time where I could change things.

These things affected my whole life in some way or another.

I was shy and always afraid. I cannot remember a time when I did not feel afraid. As an adult, I continued to feel unaccepted, misunderstood, and alone most of the time even when I was around others. As I grew older, I began to understand that my mother had challenges of her own. I always wondered, *"Would I ever have real friends who would like being around me?"* I felt as though this world was an excessively big, lonely world to live in. I learned how to isolate myself at a very young age. Because I got blamed for so many things that my sister would do, it made me feel as though my mom favored her over me. Most times, my mother would not even take the time to listen to my side. She would just say, *"I know you started it."* My sister got away with a lot of things, and this caused me to believe my mom loved her more than she loved me.

Being labeled by my mom caused me not to have much self-worth to hang on to. The distance between her and I made me feel as though there was nothing good about me. Many times, I wondered, *"Was I adopted from another family, and my real mom was out there looking for me?"* I began to feel so unloved and so unworthy. I felt as though I was wearing a sign on my forehead saying, *"I am whatever my mom says I am."* I know this is the way others will treat me. It came to a point that if someone would say something to me, I would hold on to it. I just got lost in the thought of what they said or how they just treated me. I would then be trapped there in these thoughts for hours, sometimes days, weeks, and in my self-conscious mind for years. Not realizing I had become imprisoned by my own thoughts. Holding on to words and actions of what someone else said and how they perceived who and what I was. I allowed those thoughts to play repeatedly in my mind causing me to feel so angry, I felt as though I would explode. It was like I was in this big world alone and nobody cared about me. I often wondered, *"How could they care about me if I was invisible?"*

Throughout my life, there were many times I felt feelings of guilt and shame. The warfare that I dealt with in my mind on a daily basis became part of my dreams. I believe in my mind even when I was asleep that I was fighting for my mother's and others' love and acceptance. It got so bad that at times I did not even want to go to bed. I tried to avoid sleep because I did not want to experience these horrific dreams. Some mornings I would wake up so tired in my body and mind as though I had really been in a physical fight with someone. These thoughts consumed me to the point that I did not even realize how much power and privilege I had given to what my mom and others thought of who I was or could become. I was propelled to fight in my sleep for the understanding, love and the acceptance that I was seeking for in my life.

There were times when I would hold thoughts in my mind for hours. The same thoughts would play in my mind repeatedly. Being a prisoner of my own thoughts became like an addiction. I no longer knew how to live without feeding on the pain others caused me. To forgive and forget was so hard for me. Instead, I allowed my thoughts to cause pain and imprison my mind. To my surprise, my thoughts painted a picture in my mind that held me captured. I carried condemnation over into my adulthood allowing my thoughts to become my reality. My thoughts consumed my life depriving me of being a whole person, limiting my ability to reach my divine destiny. My life became an example of Proverbs 23:7, *"So as a man thinketh in his heart, so is he."*

I was missing out on God's best for me! My thoughts kept me in the shadows of my past watching others live their lives as mine passed me by. I was just sitting on the sideline waiting for my turn to come. I was waiting for someone to notice my brokenness and give me the opportunity to be healed. Yet, I sat there too afraid to move forward, and because of fear, I was allowing my past to rob me of my future. I sat there allowing others' thoughts and opinions of me to become my own and to dictate who I was and would become. As time went by, I found myself rejecting others before they could reject me! These negative thoughts worsened overtime and became so rooted to the point that I no longer recognized the person I was because my thoughts affected my identity, ability and relationships. Now, I realize that by allowing myself to become victimized only weakens my abilities to grow and become a whole person. My thoughts consumed a lot of my precious time, and energy that I could have used to better myself as well as the life of others.

# Chapter Two
## *My School Years*

Once I started school, I felt out of place because it was extremely hard for me to fit in with my peers. Most of the time, I tried to get lost in the crowd hoping no one would notice me, and I did the same at home. As a child growing up, I always felt as though I was misunderstood by everyone. The only person I felt understood me was my baby brother. Everyone else seemed as though they did not even know I existed at home or school. I experienced this throughout my whole childhood, and some of my adult life. When I left home at the age of six to start the first grade, I was so afraid of leaving my mother and most of all my baby brother. I was constantly worrying about him although he was fine. I had been accustomed to taking care of him. Sometimes I felt like he was my own little boy. My first-grade year was harder in my eyes. I spent most of it alone and afraid of the unknown not really knowing what to expect at this place. I spent most of my time staring out of the window just waiting until it was time to go home to the place, I was familiar with although I had my fears there. Still, it was home and if nothing else, I had my baby brother and I knew he loved and needed me.

Life at home was rough although there were moments when things felt better like when my mother would take us shopping on Broad Street to pay on our layaways, and buy us popcorn at H.L. Green's Store; this was such an exciting time for me. I recall riding on the city bus, and seeing so many beautiful things and many people moving about. But when it was all over, I returned back home where I had to walk on pins and needles and try not to get blamed for something that I did not do. At school, the kids picked on me because I would cry a lot and stay to myself. There were times when I would have accidents on myself on a weekly basis. My sister would take me home and my mother would beat me with an iron cord or a belt. I would get cleaned up, change my clothes and go back to school.

Sometimes, my sister would take me to our neighborhood's store and a man in the neighborhood would buy me some cookies. Then, I would return to school. There were times when I returned to school, this girl in my class would ask for my cookies. When I said, *"no,"* she would sharpen her pencil and stick me on my legs with it. I was too afraid to tell the teacher so I just endured it. One day, her house burned down and she moved out of the neighborhood to attend another school. This made my life somewhat better. During the remainder of the school year, my life seemed to improve in some ways. I met new friends. At times, I felt normal if there was such a thing.

Time went on and I repeated the first grade. Attending the first grade was better the second time around. I was not sent home this term neither did I shy away from anyone. Mrs. Brown was my repeated first grade teacher, and boy, was she different from my soon to be second grade teacher, Mrs. English! The two were like night and day. While Mrs. Brown was not as nice and caring as Mrs. English was, I always felt she meant well. She was just being herself. I remember when she and the teacher next door would get in conflicts and go back and forth with each other. This would all boil over and they would be alright again. I did not feel very connected to Mrs. Brown or the kids in my class. Most of the time, I just sat and daydreamed. I was so spaced out into my thoughts. On one hand, I was glad to be at school. At least there, I was not beaten or felt totally isolated. On the other hand, I wanted to be home. Despite all that came with being home, it was at home where my roots were, my baby brother and my mommy. Although I did not feel close to her, she was my mother; she was a familiar face.

Second grade was a good time in my life. I had this teacher named Mrs. English. She was so pretty with very long beautiful black hair. Her spirit was mild and kind. I loved being in her class. I felt connected to her. I saw in her such a caring nature, and this is something that I had long for, for so long. I enjoyed second grade, and for once in my life, I was not afraid. Third and fourth grade was as though it did not exist because my memories are blurry. My fifth-grade year was a little exciting! I had a crush on several boys in my class, but I do not think they even noticed I was there. Boy, oh boy, was my fifth-grade teacher fine and good looking! He was also nice. While fifth grade came with some challenges, there were good looking boys all over the place! But even then, I did not fit in! Sometimes, they would give me a second look. I was not popular like the other girls. Some girls had long pretty hair, and I was a shy average girl, who was scared and lived in my own shadow. I would just sit and daydream that I had a boyfriend, we got married and I was so happy only having to come back to reality and realize it was only a dream.

During sixth and seventh grade, I began to come out of my shyness somewhat and made new friends. My sixth-grade teacher, Mr. Young, was a very strict man. He would use a tire strap and if you did not get a math problem correct, he would use that strap, and give you licks in your hands and embarrass you in front of the entire class. I had a crush on my seventh-grade teacher because he was so nice to me. His smile was out of this world! There were even a couple of boys during that time that I would have conversations with, and I really liked one of them; Billy was my favorite. He was dark chocolate and so cute; however, he was what you would call a gangster. I liked to look at him anyway. All during my elementary school term, there were negative and positive experiences which I would have loved to share with my mom. She and I did not have that kind of relationship, so I kept many of these experiences to myself. As a child, I really hated my life because everyone around me seemed so happy and fulfilled, and all I could think about was my life at home and school. At home I was the black sheep and at school I was a ghost trying to follow in someone else's footsteps.

During my eighth-grade school year, I had what some would call a puppy love experience. I thought I had a boyfriend until a different guy who wanted to date me pulled a knife out and threatened my boyfriend saying, *"I will cut you with this knife if you do not stop calling her your girlfriend, because I want her for myself."* My boyfriend became afraid of this guy, and he stated that the guy could have me. Because I was already acquainted with rejection, this situation felt like it was just another person abandoning me. I realized that my boyfriend had a legitimate reason to break away from me and to protect himself; however, this was once again in life that I felt rejected. While I was very angry with them both, as time went by, I understood that he was just afraid for his safety.

By the ninth grade and for the remainder of my high school years, I felt as if I was a female wounded from a child. Hurt and pain continued to transpire into my life as I was raped at the tender age of fifteen by someone I knew. It happened one day after school when my then supposed best friend and neighbor asked me to go with her to obtain something from a friend's house. She assured me that we would not be there long, so against my better judgment knowing that if I got home late my mom would surely punish me, I went alone with her anyway. Soon after, we arrived inside of the house where we were to stop in for a few minutes to pick up her belongings and leave.

When we walked in the house her boyfriend came out from the back of the house. She followed him to the back where he came from. Immediately, his cousin came out from the front room to my right. I recognized him from school. I always thought he was cute, but never thought he would give me a second look. Now, here I was standing in his living room. He smiled at me and before I knew what was happening, he had me in his bedroom pulling off my clothes. It happened so fast, and I did not realize what was going on until I felt the horrible pain of him forcing himself on me. I began to cry while trying to push him off of me. He said to me, *"I thought this is what you came for."*

Apparently, my friend, her boyfriend and cousin knew what was supposed to take place, but no one thought enough about my feelings to let me know, so that I could have at least had a choice in the matter. I was so devastated. Here my virginity was taken from me without my consent in the worst way imaginable. I left there in a state of shock. I was in pain, embarrassed, angry with my friend, her boyfriend and his cousin. Whatever I thought I liked about him changed. I felt so betrayed, I did not see this coming. I felt so violated, dirty and ashamed. Now on top of that, I was afraid of what my mother would do when I got home.

Once I got home, there she was. As soon as I walked in the house, she started swinging the belt in my direction with no questions asked. No time to explain what happened to me. There I stood already in pain and injured. Now, she was adding insult to injury making a bad situation even worse. I really wanted to tell her that I had just got raped. Here I was in so much agony, and no one to comfort me. I know that I broke her rule getting home late. But I believe that if I could have talked to my mother or someone at that time, I would have not been so hard on myself for trusting in someone I thought was my friend and blaming myself for what happen to me. This incident caused me to isolate myself and not really trust anyone. Following the rape, and long after I lost all interest in school but I continued to attend my classes. I just could not seem to focus on my studies. My teacher would be up teaching, and I would not hear a thing he or she said to me. I only saw their lips moving. All of the pain caused me to have a lack of attention in school. Soon enough the bell would ring, and it was time to move to the next class period. The same thing would take place in each class. At the end of the school day, I would begin to think about going home. My thoughts often were, *"What will I get blamed for today? I am just not in the mood for this. I am so tired of this life."* Once reality would sit in, I would realize that I had nowhere else to go except home. After continuing to lose focus and experiencing pure boredom, I just stopped going to school against my father's wishes. I stopped going, and got a job. Later, I got my G.E.D. Years later, I enrolled into Georgia Military College.

## Chapter Three
# *My First and Second Marriage*

Once I was out of high school, I began my first real relationship with my daughter's father, Hamp. I was the last child to leave home, so I was very anxious to leave my mother's home to experience my own family. When I met Hamp, I thought I had met my Prince Charming because he charmed me into thinking that he and I would live happily ever after; however, I soon found out that our lives were far from a fairytale. My fairytale relationship with him became more like a pure nightmare. After a month of a loving and close relationship, he came to me and said, *"The honeymoon is over."* This is when the nightmare began! Following these words, he stayed out all night. He arrived home the next day with no valid explanation or remorse. Months later,

I found out I was pregnant; I was now not only a new wife, but also soon to be a new mother.

Following our daughter's birth, I thought that things between him and I would get better. After all, he seemed happy that we were having a baby! Once she was born, he seemed even more excited for a while. It was good between us in some ways. Suddenly, all hell broke loose; he completely changed. My husband started leaving home and would not come back until the next day. After he stayed out for one night, he would stay out for two nights, three nights, or four nights at a time or even longer. His behavior progressed. In the beginning, I called the emergency room, funeral home, police department, and family members trying to rule out if something bad had happened to him. After a while, I just stopped calling places looking for him.

I watched my mother stay with my father for years even with him drinking and cheating on her with another woman, and even sometimes becoming violent toward her. Because my mother stayed in her marriage, I thought I could endure marital affairs, mental abuse and other problems caused by my husband. I loved him. He was my daughter's father, and the first real relationship that I had ever experienced. I did not date in high school, so when I met Hamp, I thought I had found true love. After all, I did not have a picture or concept of how real love looked or felt; I had never seen love exemplified in the house where I grew up because none was shown. At least, none which I could identify.

Hamp swept me right off my feet. He was a very handsome

man who seemed to be head over heels in love with me. We met during a time in my life when I desperately needed and wanted to be loved. He knew all of the right words to say! Although I was beautiful, young, and very kind, my husband seemed to prefer the company of others over me. Because of this, I began to feel insecure and rejected. Again, I found myself feeling alone which caused me to question my self-worth wondering, *"What was wrong with me?"* I soon discovered that infidelity and disrespect were not the only things keeping my husband out there in the street away from his family for days at a time. I later found out that he had a substance addiction.

Having this information did not make me feel any better, nor did it ease my pain and loneliness. I stayed in this marriage for about three to four years, and because I was alone so much, I decided to leave the state. I thought my absence from our home would help heal my heart or help ease the pain. I was out of the state when I received the news of his death. My daughter, Therese and I arrived back in Georgia to carry out his funeral arrangements, and we decided to stay. Once again, I experienced grief and loss. During the time of his passing, my biggest fear was what my daughter may have felt or would have to overcome. For example, my thoughts were, *"My daughter will not get to know and spend time with her father. What would this loss be like for her? How will she feel about not having her father in her life? What effect will his death have on a female growing up?"* Although this situation was devastating, we got through it. I accepted the Lord in my life when my daughter's father died. We attended church services every Sunday, and I had so much peace and joy building a relationship with my Savior, but just as

Adam felt alone without Eve, I too, felt alone at times. I wanted a companion and a father for my daughter.

Five years later, I met my two sons' father, Joe. I was a single mom hoping one day to remarry and have more children. My daughter wanted a sister! I lived next door to Joe's friend and one day, while I was over his house, I met Joe. I saw him after that on regular visits when he would come next door. He was attractive and seemed nice. Joe asked me for a date; after several times of him asking, I decided to go out with him. We dated for a while and separated for a season. I saw and heard some things I did not particularly like but I had chosen to ignore and disregard them. I was young, naive and I thought that I needed a husband and a father for my daughter and our future children. After about two years, Joe and I got married. As time progressed, I began to have many regrets about marrying or even taking a second look at this man.

Joe's mean and controlling nature would not allow him to be sensitive and caring. I loved my children so much, and I felt that I could not properly care for them on my own. I did not think it was fair to them not to have a mother and father. I felt as though I was not strong enough to parent alone. I was a young woman in my twenties trying to be a mother and a wife. At times, it seemed as though I did not have any time for myself. My husband would often isolate himself; he found a space in the house, and went there to shut all of us out.

At times, he seemed to have been very angry with life! He became very short tempered with me and his children. There

**Finally Free!**
*I Was a Prisoner of My Own Thoughts.*

were times when we would make plans to go out with just the two of us, and he would just cancel them at a moment's notice. Whenever he would take the children and I out to lunch or dinner, he would always complain about the price. Once he would finish eating his food, he was ready to leave without being patient enough to let us finish. Right there in front of the children and I, he showed no remorse. He was the kind of man who thought, *"children should be seen not heard."* Our time together was not all bad. There were times, here and there, we laughed and really enjoyed each other. I remember my sister kept the kids for us and we went out of town to his niece's graduation, and we got along well. We laughed and had so much fun. There were times when he looked at me, I could see the love he had for me in his eyes. He would sometimes share with me about his childhood. He did not get along well with his mother, but he always spoke highly of his father.

Joe was there when I had our two sons, and he helped me take care of them when they were babies. He changed diapers, fed them and clothed them. He loved us in his own way. Coming from a family and formal marriage where there was none, or little love and closeness shown I really thought this was a step up. It was the closest to it I had ever had. I was looking for love and acceptance and I thought this was what it looked like. I heard love was blind, so I just did not see or I ignored his faults as I chose to pray for his needs. He was the father of my children and there were good moments in our relationship. He was often stubborn and in denial, so this would cause problems for us. I wanted to belong and be loved and needed. I would still try and keep the peace in our relationship and home.

As time went on, we seemed to grow apart. I suggested going to counseling, but that was not going to take place, not in this lifetime, so I thought. Later, as time passed by to my surprise, he agreed to go to counseling. I thought for a while it was going well; however, one day, he said he did not need anyone telling him how to treat his wife. He stated he knew how to treat me. He often said if I take what he gives, maybe I would get what I really wanted. I believed because he never had a good relationship with his mother, he failed to value my opinions and feelings. I remember him telling me one day after we had gone to a counseling session, *"A woman cannot tell a man nothing. All she is good for is the kitchen and the bedroom."* After this statement, he ended the counseling sessions.

I loved him. Sometimes, I felt as though I could not or would not live without him in my life. I realize now that I felt that way because I was used to him. We had soul ties; these soul ties are not that easy to be broken as easy as some may think. It took lots of praying and time to break this soul tie. Throughout the years, we would have a big blow out and separate for a short while. Then, he and I would get right back together. It was hard for both of us to be apart from each other. I think in our own way, Joe and I genuinely loved and cared for each other; however, we were not compatible enough to make our marriage work. Our outlook on the way a marriage should be was just too off course. We both came from brokenness, and as time went on, we really began to go downhill. There were several times when I thought of leaving him. Because of my feelings for him even after the children were out on their own, I kept holding on.

I held on to my spiritual beliefs that if I kept praying, I would get the answers I needed to lead me in the right direction. Although I prayed a lot, I was so mentally and emotionally drained. I do not think I knew the difference in what I was feeling compared to what God was saying to me. In other words, I wondered, *"How much of my thoughts were Godly or of the flesh?"* I would look at Joe and see right through him. At times, I would look at him and did not even recognize who he was. My husband became like a stranger to me. We divorced, but continued living together on two different sides of the house. Sometimes we would not see or talk to each other for three days or longer although we lived in the same house. It came to a point that the idea of regaining what we had seemed so distant to the point of no return. We had been together for so long and gotten so use to each other that neither one of us wanted to be the first to say goodbye although we both were aware of the stagnation and declining in our relationship. I made a decision to stop lying to myself and face reality. I searched deeply but I had nothing left to give to this relationship. I gave it all I had, and despite my efforts, no matter how hard I tried, I kept coming up empty. I just could not find any more strength or reason to continue. I loved and cared for him for so many years, and it was never my intention to leave him behind. It just came to a point that I had to lose him to find myself.

## Chapter Four
# *Life As a Mother and Grandmother*

Although I experienced many challenges, my life was good as a mother. With my first child,Therese I was in labor for twenty- two hours with her, and oh boy was that a rough time! I gave birth to her when I was twenty years old. She was born a beautiful baby girl with beautiful hair. I would dress her up, and sit her in the corner of the sofa just to look at her because she was so beautiful and innocent. She became my inspiration. Once I sat her on the sofa, she would be sitting there not even knowing she was in this world. When she became old enough to talk, she would at times go and get my Bible. She would already have turned to the scripture; she would tell me to read God's Word to her. It is ironic that the very scriptures she wanted me to read to her were really meant to give me peace for whatever I was facing that day or week. Therese was my little angel, and I learned so much from her.

As she got older, she spent a lot of time in her playroom where she only wanted to work with papers. Sometimes, I would try to entertain her with toys, but toys were not a big deal to her. All she wanted was for me to give her papers and a snack. After doing so, she would be okay. It was she and I for a while after her father passed. We spent a lot of time going to church and visiting my family. Once she started school, it was hard for her but as time went on, she got better. With the loss of her father at such a young age, I often wondered what thoughts were going through her head. Therese always wanted to help me out around the house.

Eight years after Therese's birth, I gave birth to my second child, Sebastian born from my second husband and I. Sebastian was so precious! My delivery of him was not hard at all, and the labor time was not as long. My son grew up always being curious about learning even at the tender age of four. I recall him saying to my daughter and I, *"Teach me everything you know because I want to be smart and become a doctor when I grow up."* Sebastian grew up always reading or learning about something new! He loved saving his money. There were many times he was ill and hospitalized. Because of this, he missed days from school. Yet, Sebastian did not stop striving for the best. During times when he was hospitalized, he would ask me to pray with him.

Prayers gave us both the strength we needed to stay strong

and endure the time he spent hospitalized. He once told me that I was the closest thing to God that he had ever known and that I was a wise woman. Sebastian wanted to learn from me, and this touched my heart! That young boy does not know just how much he touched my life and all the lessons he taught me. He always talked about learning from me but he inspired me. Through his encouragement, I am now writing my first book. After working on this book, it has awakened the gift of the writer in me. I know if I live long enough by the grace of God, I shall write many books. As a child growing up, and throughout his school years, I often worried about him a lot. When he went off to college, it was very hard for me at first because I always worried about him and his well-being, but God kept him, and gave me peace. I continue to keep him in my prayers, and when we talk on the phone or visit each other, I pray with him. We share whatever is going on in our lives with each other. The Lord has been faithful to the promises that he gave concerning my son. He promised me that his adult life would be better than his childhood.

Two years following Sebastian's birth, I gave birth to my second son, Lionel. I had dry labor with him, and that was pain like no other. Lionel gave me a fit as he made his way into this world. Even as a child, he was always a busy little boy, but oh so sweet! I remember grabbing him just so I could kiss his jaws and hold him close so he would know he was loved. I really wanted him to know his mother loved him because he always seemed to be trying to get attention. He was always in something or another. Lionel was a very curious child. As a little boy, he climbed on the counter top of the bathroom and got my clock down off the wall as though he wanted to see what made it work.

Lionel came into this world wanting to explore it! He would get things and tear them apart, then put them back together again. I often told him he should become a computer engineer because he was so good at computers. Lionel once took a computer apart and put it back together again with no help from anyone. I loved and cared for him. He was my baby, and the last child I would have. Lionel looked like me and regardless of how others saw him, I know he was a good child. He was often misunderstood but mommy loved her baby. I remember when he was a little boy and his brother and sister would send him to my room for some reason or another, and I would just let him in and we spent time together. My baby joined a baseball team. I was so proud of him. Later, he joined the football team at his high school. Once he graduated from high school, he got accepted into a college. Again, I was overjoyed of his accomplishments. As much as I tried to get close to him, he never really opened up completely, and he held a lot of his thoughts inside. It was like he was just in a world of his own.

Today, all of my children are adults. Therese has children of her own. I really miss her as a little girl. While we were so close, she is now older. I know that the training and love I gave her will guide her in the direction of her purpose. Sebastian's life as an adult is so much better than it was growing up. He is now a licensed psychologist, choreographer, motivational speaker and an author; he is currently working on his second book. Lionel also has a family of his own. I decided even before my children were born that I would try my hardest to give them the love, encouragement and support that I felt I missed out on and let them know how much I loved them on a daily basis. That is what I set out to do. Before they came along, I never knew I could love someone so much and have such a strong bond. With all my children, I played an active role in their lives from being a class mom in their elementary school, reading to the classes, praying with my children, teaching them about their creator, going on field trips to having birthday parties at their schools and taking them to the library for summer reading programs. I tried to love and protect them the best way I knew how. Throughout their middle and high school years, I would pick them up from after school events and support them in their interests.

Despite hard times, disappointments, and issues in both of my marriages, my love for my children kept me going. When life got so unbearable that I felt like I could not or would not make it, the thought of my three children needing me gave me the motivation and drive to pray and hold on. I did not get the love, encouragement and support I needed from my parents and my children's fathers. When I looked into their eyes and thought about how their very survival depended on me being there for them, loving, caring and supporting them, it gave me the strength and courage I needed to press on. I did everything within my power and strength to give my children the love, encouragement and support that I longed for. Although I was not a perfect mom, I loved my children despite everything else going on in my life. My children were the center of my attention, and their well-being was my top priority. If I failed them in any way, it was not intentional because my children were always what I treasured the most.

## *My children and I*

I was not only blessed to birth and raise my children, but also God allowed me to live and experience the joy of being a grandmother. The time I spend with my grandchildren is a joy and pleasure! We often had prayer time and I enjoyed teaching them about God, their creator, and how to pray and trust in Him. I remember even having lunch with them at their school and my oldest granddaughter's class birthday party. I also had the opportunity to visit my baby son's house and spend time with his sons and at times with the oldest son at the movie theater.

I thank God for the opportunity to have had a chance to spend time with them. Although I did not get to do much as I would have loved to do with them, I thank God for the time I was allowed. My prayers are always going up for them that their future will be bright! I always pray that God will bless them. I had the pleasure of spending time with them all except my son's daughter for circumstances beyond my control, but that's how life works sometimes, so you accept what you cannot change and move forward. You cannot stay stuck in the past, so I have come to terms with it, and continue to pray for better times.

*My Grandchildren*

# Chapter Five
## *My Parents' Life and Death*

My mother suffered a lot of heartaches and pain in her marriage with my father. As a child and sometimes even as an adult, I thought it was normal. I literally thought that *"till death do us part"* meant you were supposed to be in a marriage for better or worse and that is what my mother did. I even tried to get her away from it if only for a while, but she refused to leave her home. She really believed that and so she stayed until her death. My mother had a heart condition from all of the worrying and stress she endured with my father's drinking, infidelity and just being mean.

I experienced emotional stress from my mother's death. It affected me quite differently than my father's death. I cried for her! My mother knew so many people. Her funeral was packed. Some people had to be on the outside grounds of the church. Before my mom died, I got a chance to be close to her. Although the closeness was not in the way I needed when I was a child, but we developed a better relationship once I was older. She and I talked often, went out to eat and shop. During the time I was pregnant with my oldest son, she bought me Chinese food and we would go back to my apartment to eat and take a nap. I really enjoyed the time she and I spent together; however, my mom's health condition got worse and she was hospitalized.

During her hospitalization, I visited her. As I looked over at her, thoughts went through my mind. I watched the woman whom I had known all my childhood and early adult life now laying in a hospital bed fighting for her life. I wished she and I had more time to make up for all of the moments I felt we lost while I was growing up. My mom appeared to be so out of my reach, and for me to help her situation was out of my control. Here she lies so helpless, and despite what she did or did not do for me or to me as a child, this was my mother lying there and I loved her. As I looked into her eyes, I could see her appearing to drift away. I wanted to stay with her through the night, but I had just given birth to my youngest son, Lionel. I was still recovering, and I needed to return home to care for him. I thought about her all through the night. The next day, I was told that she had passed away. From that day to this one, it seemed as if my entire world changed. While we were not as close as I would have desired us to be, I loved my mother and now she was gone! The bond between a mother and her child is one that will last a lifetime. The connection will always exist physically, mentally and emotionally.

On the day of my father's funeral, I watched my siblings as they really seemed to be having a hard time. As my sister began to speak about our father, I realized it was real for her because their relationship was close. My sister and father spent timeless moments together. She cared for him, and he cared for her. The two bonded as a daughter and father should. My sister and father shared a house for years with my mom before she died; my father and I never shared that type of relationship. During my father's final days, he lived with my brother, and they shared timeless moments. My father's death appeared to have been a great loss to my brother and sister and maybe even to the rest of my siblings. However, I saw it in an entirely different way as I sat there at his grave site outside on that cold rainy winter day. As I looked around at everyone, all I could think of was how cold I was and wanted it to all be over with, so I could go home to my warm apartment and get from around all these strange people. My siblings and I do not have the closeness most siblings have, and I think it is because of our parents' lack of demonstration.

In our home, closeness, love and unity was almost non-existent which as a child I felt I desperately needed. Because we did not have much of an example to follow, my father's absence did not feel much different from his presence while I was growing up. After his funeral, my siblings and I went our separate ways although I will never give up hope for these circumstances to change, and for us to have a closer bond. Nine months after my father's funeral on November 14, 2021 around 5:30 A.M, I had a dream about my father. In this dream, I found myself in a stranger's house whose last name was Jones. The family appeared to resemble my father, and I mentioned to them that my father's last name was Jones. I continued to explain that my father was also from the same county as they were. As they were talking among themselves, I began to think about my father and right there in my sleep, I began to cry. At that moment, I realized I was grieving for him.

I tried and wanted to get to know him, but for some reason it just did not seem to work. There was so much distance between my father and I, the man I grew up all of my childhood, visited and talked to on the phone as an adult. Still, I never really felt close to him. During this dream, I wept for him and deeply wished I genuinely knew him. The thoughts I carried for so long of feeling neglected by him as though I was of no importance to him as a child or adult, just would not allow me to see him any different until after he was gone. I now feel the connection. I understand and regret that so many moments have gone, and I will never get them back. While crying and grieving in my dream, I awakened and realized I was still crying and grieving for my father. For the first time after my father's funeral, I felt the lost.

*My father, siblings and I*

# Chapter Six
## *Turning Point in My Life*

I spent a lot of time focusing on past situations, choices and events that took place in my life wishing I could go back to a place in time where I could change things. Now, I realize how it would have benefited me more to stop looking back at what I should or could have done. I realize all of the precious time I spent living out my past repeatedly not only stagnated my life, but also caused me to become trapped in my own mind, ceasing to fully develop into the woman I now know I can be. I became stuck in a set of routines that kept me from moving forward.

I realize now that it was not my parents or the people of the past holding me back. Instead, it was my very own thoughts robbing and limiting me from moving forward. My very thoughts were now determining my actions! Even when I came to the realization of what had taken place, I knew that it was not going to be easy to break free. I knew that I would have to go through a process. It was a process getting here, and there will be a process going forward. As a child, I never realized that harboring negative feelings would cause me so much lost in my life later. The negative emotions rolled over into my adult life from thoughts of my childhood. Among everyone's opinions, I never had a say in any of our family matters. After realizing how this negativity grew internally and began to show up in my day-to-day life, I knew I had to fight like hell to break free!

Each new relationship I entered became a feeding ground for more abuse. Hurt stemmed as I reflected on the thoughts that I was not good enough to be loved by my mother and father. The two people I loved and depended on for everything, for my very survival. Doubt and insecurity showed up in every relationship or situation I encountered causing me to question my self-worth. I never felt like I fit in anywhere or with anybody. If I had a friend, I would feel left out because I felt they gave someone else more attention than they gave me. I felt like I had to compete, as though I was in a race for attention.

Over a period of time, this type of behavior wore me out mentally. Reality came into play, and I realized that I was not stuck here. I was just committed to this behavior pattern for so long it seemed like the only thing that kept me sane, but I realized I had to let go of this because it had become more harmful than helpful. Looking back at my past life and behavior, I realized the reason I could not move forward was because I kept applying the old formula to a new level in my life, and that I had to change the old to get a new and different result. I had to learn a new and better way to deal with things. My deep desire to be loved and accepted led me to make negative choices in my relationships. I was trying to be what others wanted me to be, just to be accepted, to feel wanted and needed. Throughout my life, this became my pattern.

Both my parents grew up in a strict household where they were seen but not heard. I realized now they did the best they could with the abilities they had to work with from their past childhood and adult life, and what they both brought into the marriage. I tried to think, *"What their childhood was like, what things they were deprived of?" "What abuse did they suffer at someone else's hand?" "What were their lives like before I came along?" "What were their prisons?" "What were they afraid of?" "What causes them to lose hope?"* In every family, there are past experiences that determine the outcome of their future, whether it be positive or negative. It is how each person in their family conceives and utilizes them, determines the outcome of what picture they will paint for their future lives.

Regardless of how much love may or may not be shown, each child's personality is different. I realize now that they did the best they could with what they were working with. Being a parent is not an easy job and there was no manual for them to go by. With the day-to-day responsibilities they had to deal with and the limited provisions that were provided for them as African-Americans. With their educational level, they would not have understood a manual anyway. Even now in the 21st century we live in as parents, we still struggle to be the best parents we can possibly be to our children. And still at times fall short. The reality is that the family is the basic unit in which we all grow up in, so whether we want it or not, it leaves a very similar impression. In fact, while forming a new family, we often follow the same patterns that we have learned from our childhood whether they are right or wrong.

It was only when I accepted the Lord Jesus Christ as my savior and built a relationship with him that the process of healing and deliverance began to take place in my life. It allowed me to discover my self-worth, and understand how to build a healthy relationship with myself and others. Because of the deep hold that my thoughts once had over me, it has taken some time to operate in a new way of thinking. It took many years and wrong choices to accept and embrace the beautiful, loving person who I and others have come to know! Now, I choose to take my past fears, hurts, disappointments and use them in a positive way to help others. In the past, I loved and cared for so many people, but loving and caring for myself was so much harder for me to do. I learned that for me to grow into the beautiful woman who I have longed to become, I would have to discover my true self. I knew inside of me was a woman full of possibilities, hopes and dreams! I found ways to allow my past hurts to be a positive tool to empower others. I see myself walking in the fullness of my destiny surrounded by the people, places, and things that have been waiting for my arrival.

I spent so much time looking back, and dragging the weight of past thoughts, hurts, disappointments, and shame. I listened to them playing over and over again in my mind beating myself up; I never felt good enough. These feelings almost took me out. I was bound to what I had become. Holding on to past thoughts and events drained me of my energy. I am now wiser. I can see clearer now the blinders are off and the chains have been broken. I am stronger now; I've walked through the prison doors to freedom. All charges against me have been dropped. Glory, Hallelujah! My best days are in front of me!

# Chapter Seven
## *A Love Letter To The Girl Inside of Me*

I am writing this love letter to you to let you know that I am very proud of you! I want to let you know that you were not alone although at the time, you may have felt that you were. God and the angels he assigned to watch over you were right there fighting with you to keep you sane, holding on with you so you would not give up or harm yourself in any way. Psalms 34:7 (NIV) *"The Angel of the Lord encamps around those who fear Him, and He delivers them."*

As you travel on this journey called life, I realize what a rough time you had being a child. You often carried such a heavy load, and it left you feeling tired and devastated, the thought of being disconnected from the two people who you relied on the most.

But you have survived through it all! Hold your head up now; you no longer have to hold it down. Do not be afraid anymore. No one is going to hurt you. 2 Timothy 1:7 "For God has not given you the spirit of fear, but the spirit of power of love and a sound disciplined mind."

Little girl, if you open your mouth and speak now someone will listen. You know longer have to be afraid of being knocked down for letting someone know how you feel. You can also lose the fear of the rodents and bugs that tormented you. You do not live in that place any more. You have moved on. I know how you often worried about fitting in, wanting to love someone and that person returning that same kind of love back to you. Well, that prince found you and took you away from it all and loves you unconditionally. He loves you with the Agape love and this is the highest form of love one can experience; it never fails. That gentle person you longed for and friend you never had. The love and acceptance you wanted, you have now.

I am so proud of you that you have moved on and stopped concerning yourself with what other people thought, said, or did to you. Now, as I take up where you left off, I have decided to put the hurt, fear, disappointments, rejection, and shame you endured for so many years in the past where it belongs, so that I can enjoy and fully embrace a healthy future. What you endured for so many years was no fault of your own. It was the life you were born in, and the family you were given. I want to assure you that I'm no longer in that prison where my thoughts held me captivated for so long. Jesus saved me and freed me. I now, let go of the anger and rage we both felt and were engaged in from time to time. We were in that mind prison for so many years. I am so much stronger now as an adult. I can and will do all things through Christ who strengthens me!

I now have the power and courage to cast down these imaginations and high thoughts that try to exalt itself above the Word of God. I now bring them into captivity and not allow them to imprison me as they did you although they still try. You can be proud of what and who you have become. I am now a beautiful and intelligent woman and can hold my own. Nobody is pushing me around. I cast all my cares on God because He cares for me. Now through Him, I control the thoughts that come to my mind and determine which ones I will accept and which ones I will not accept. With His grace and mercy, I can now forget those things which are behind me and press toward the prize of the high calling that's before me in Christ Jesus. When you were a child, you were limited to what you could do or say about your situation. But now as an adult I have a choice and a voice, therefore I will open my mouth and speak for us, and we will be heard. At times it seemed that my best days were over, that I was too old, that time had passed me by.

But now I know that it had nothing to do with my age but the desire, passion, and the ability to embrace what's in front of me. And that although it was delayed, we were not forgotten. The Lord said in His Word that you were chosen while yet in our mother's womb and that He would never leave us nor forsake us. What the enemy meant for our harm Our Creator took and used it for our good!

Now, little girl inside of me, I am now that grown woman that you have become. You suffered so long in silence. You endured so much pain, disappointment, and shame, when all you wanted was to be loved and appreciated. You can now let go of it and let God have it! Allow him to turn it around for our good and get the glory from all of it. What you suffered was not in vain, it will be used as a tool to heal other hurting people. Thank you for bringing me this far, I am now strong enough to carry us on to the finish line. When I get there, I will not forget to let you out to shout and rejoice with me!

What you have gone through and fought so hard for will be counted because God's Word says all things are working together for the good of those that love the Lord and that is called for His purpose. If you would have given up, I would not have been here and had the opportunity to live out my destiny and help others. I thought I missed my moment in time. I thought the clock for my life had stopped or slowed down years ago. But by the grace of God and His tender mercy when I sought Him with my whole heart, I found Him and He reset my clock. He gave me some more time to get off the side line and run the race He set before me. I was designed to fulfill the plan He chose for me while I was yet in my mother's womb. I am off that sideline now where I sat for years allowing my thoughts to dictate my every move. I am on the track running the race, being that strong, beautiful, and determined woman you fought so hard for me to become.

Little girl, you pushed me forward so that I could embrace my destiny! It has been in front of me all the time waiting on me to leap.

To take ownership of every opportunity that is set before me to dream, build, and become that Wise Master Builder. I am no longer afraid of my own shadow or looking for approval and acceptance from others, the stagnation is gone.

I embrace greatness. I now see myself for the first-time in my life really expecting greatness. There is something out there waiting for me that is greater than you or I could ever imagine. I give myself permission to embrace it, as I walk in the new-found freedom and all the possibilities it has to offer me. I rejoice in our Creator and see his face and allow him to order my steps right into my destiny, to a place where there is freedom in a place where I will live and accept myself and all that I will become. As I continue this journey that you began of self-love and self-discovery, I now realize just how hard you were on yourself, overloading your mind with the heavy weight of thoughts. The past is now behind me, and I embrace my future.

The future you fought so hard for me to have I now have and that is where I choose to be. No more allowing others to dictate my life. I choose me and take the weight of others and my past thoughts and opinions off my mind. There is only one voice I am listening to now! (John 10:4-5) My sheep knows my voice and a stranger he will not follow. Nothing can stop me now but me. I stop beating up on myself for whom and what I and others thought I should have been, and focus on the now, where I am and where I am headed. There are greater things that are waiting for us when we get there, I say us because little girl you will always be a part of me. I will continue to fight for all you fought for to get us to where we are today. No more boundaries here. I let go of all the negative thoughts from my mind. I take a deep breath and I am here. In a world full of possibilities, no limits, no boundaries, all things are possible because I know this is where I was meant to be. Now, little girl inside of me you can come out to play and know that it is okay. God has made a way and this is where we will stay. Nothing is standing in our way.

We are here now standing tall, as we accept the call. We move forward, being the best that we can be. I sense the greatness inside of me that's been waiting to come out, longing to be free. So, I take a deep breath and I suck it all in like a sponge. I absorb it all. I allow my mind to travel to places where we both have dreamed of being, and suddenly we are here. I look outside my window, and I see the leaves blowing on the trees and they look so free! And right then tears began to roll from the corners of my eyes, and I found myself filled with such amazement. They appear not to have a care in the world. So, I close my eyes and leap into the now. I am here in my future.

I give myself permission to be that person I was always meant to be! I hear destiny calling. I embrace it. I am finally here, where I have always longed to be.

*BEING ME;*
*FREE!!!!!!!!!!!!!!!!!!!!!*

*Ray and I.*
*He is my Prince Charming.*

Made in the USA
Columbia, SC
06 October 2022

68772456R00031